# WOMEN MENTORING WOMEN

## STUDENT GUIDE

## By Cris Jacobs

WOMEN MENTORING WOMEN

ISBN: 9798730830134

# DEDICATION

To my mother, Carol Mason, who has always been
my greatest role model. Your legacy of love
has enveloped many.

# TABLE OF CONTENTS

# ACKNOWLEDGMENTS

I want to start by thanking my husband, Danny, whose love and patience while I spent hours typing away at the keyboard was so appreciated. God blessed me with you.

Thank you to my proofreaders, cheer leaders and punctuation experts, Teresa Devlin and Pastor Donna Clark. I could not have a better team than the two of you.

Thank you to my daughter, Tarah Herbert, for sharing her beautiful artwork for the book cover.

And thank you to Pastor C.J. Plogger, for asking me to write this study, and believing that I could.

In days gone by, little girls grew up surrounded by not only their immediate family, but extended family as well. Church also holding a central place in their lives. They could learn about life and how to navigate through its seasons by watching and following the examples modeled by their mothers, grandmothers, aunts, cousins, and sisters. Watching how those women grew as they handled failures, endured struggles, and celebrated triumphs were priceless lessons.

Today, girls may not have the opportunity to experience the examples and guidance of mature women. Families don't live in a tight community as they once did or make church the priority that it should be. Women, no matter their age, need the support, friendship, guidance, and community of other women. Their loving presence in our lives encourages us, trains us, disciplines us. May this study be a step in taking the initiative to be the loving support to a woman who desires to grow and learn.

*Women Mentoring Women* is a six-month study where a mentor will teach a woman how to become the Godly woman that God intends her to be.

It is divided into four sections: <u>Listing</u>, <u>Learning</u>, <u>Leading</u>, and <u>Legacy</u>.

In the <u>Listing</u> section, a woman defines herself and learns who she is and what is important to her.

In the <u>Learning</u> section, a woman will dig deeper and realize the importance of growing, both as a woman and closer to God.

In the <u>Leading</u> section. a woman will be taught the responsibilities and duties of being a Godly woman and the impact she makes on the world around her.

In the <u>Legacy</u> section, a woman is directed to see how others are not only affected by her story but also have their lives improved.

Each section is divided into six-week lessons. Each lesson has five days of work and the student is encouraged to take Sunday and another day of their choice off.

It is highly recommended that the mentor and the student meet once a week to go over the weekly material. If that is not possible then it is encouraged they meet no later than every two weeks. If need be, they could talk over the phone or through email, but this would be a last resort as the importance of personally connecting is vital.

On the first day of every week, a student will evaluate where she sees herself, physically, emotionally, and spiritually. One being not good and ten being the best. This will provide an opportunity for the mentor to meet the student where she is and lead her to growth.

As the mentor, in the beginning of your relationship with your student, you may need to take the initiative for a short time to keep faithful to the study. If the student falls behind or "life happens," then take a short break but get started back as soon as you are able.

All scripture is from the New International Version Bible. Following the scripture in the Mentor Guide is an application that helps the mentor tie in the scripture verse with the question.

The mentor will pour themselves into the student which will build up both involved. It is a high honor to mentor someone and needs to be done with much prayer for guidance and wisdom. *Women Mentoring Women* is an opportunity for two women of God to connect, learn from each other, and draw nearer to God.

# Knowing Myself

## Part One

## Week One

## Expectations of a Woman

# Week One - Knowing Myself

<u>Day One</u>

*Expectations of a woman.*

*While that perfectly airbrushed picture can be beautiful, it can't be the standard or the scale in which we determine our beauty. The pressure on women to suck it in, color those roots, or add a filter is over the top in our society. Women can have unrealistic expectations of what true beauty is when inundated with the media and images we take in on a daily basis.*

1. What do you think makes a woman beautiful?

_____

_____

_____

_____

Write out Proverbs 31:30

_____

_____

2. Do you struggle with feelings that you "don't measure up" on the beauty scale?

_____

_____

_____

Write out Genesis 1:27

_____

_____

3. How important is "inner beauty"?

_____

_____

Write out 1 Peter 3:3-4

_____

_____

4. Describe yourself in ten words.

_____

_____

_____

Write out Psalm 139:14

_____

_____

At the beginning of each week, you will rate yourself concerning these areas – where you are physically, where you are emotionally, and where you are spiritually.

Physically- 1 2 3 4 5 6 7 8 9 10

Emotionally- 1 2 3 4 5 6 7 8 9 10

Spiritually- 1 2 3 4 5 6 7 8 9 10

# Week One- Knowing Myself

<u>Day Two</u>

*What is important to me?*

1. What gives me value?

_____
_____
_____

Write out Psalm 139:13

_____
_____

2. How do I like to spend my time?

_____
_____
_____

Write out 1 Corinthians 10:31

_____
_____

3. What would I miss if it were gone?

_____
_____
_____

Write out 2 Corinthians 4:18.

_____
_____

4. What traits of other women impress you?

_____
_____
_____

Write out Proverbs 31:25

_____

_____

# Week One – Knowing Myself

<u>Day Three</u>

*What do I believe about myself?*

*It is not always easy standing up for our beliefs. No one likes the feeling of being the odd one out. But we can't stay quiet. Someone was bold enough to share with us. Historically, women have been sharing the good news since Jesus met the woman at the well.*

1. What do I believe my role is in my family?

_____

_____

_____

Write out Romans 10:13-14

_____

_____

2. What do I believe my role is at my job and working at home?

_____

_____

_____

Write out Colossians 3:17

_____

_____

3. What do I believe is my role in society?

_____

_____

_____

Write out  Mark 12:30-31

_____

_____

4. Do I always stand up for my beliefs?

_____
_____
_____

Write out  Proverbs 8:7

_____
_____

# Week One – Knowing Myself

<u>Day Four</u>

*What do I need to work on?*

*Growing spiritually begins with a plan. We don't want to be spiritual babies. Instead, we should want to age spiritually just like we age physically.*

1. Do I know the areas in my life that I need to work on?

_____

_____

_____

Write out  2 Peter 3:18

_____

_____

2. What areas of my life do I need to work on physically?

_____

_____

_____

Write out Jeremiah 12:2

_____

_____

3. What areas of my life do I need to work on emotionally?

_____

_____

_____

Write out Luke 17:5

_____

_____

4. What areas of my life do I need to work on spiritually?

_____

_____

_____

Write out  Hebrews 6:1

_____

_____

# Week One – Knowing Yourself

Day Five

*How can I specifically improve?*

*We have all heard the saying, "If you fail to plan then you plan to fail."*

1. Do you have a plan to improve the areas in your life talked about on day 4?

_____

_____

_____

Write out  3 John 1:2

_____

_____

2. What is your plan to improve physically?

_____

_____

_____

Write out 1 Corinthians 3:16

_____

_____

3. What is your plan to improve emotionally?

_____

_____

_____

Write out  Psalm 55:4

_____

_____

4. What is your plan to grow spiritually?

_____

_____

_____

Write out 1 Peter 2:2-3

_____

_____

# Knowing Myself

## Part One

## Week Two

## Abundant Living

# Week Two - Abundant Living

<u>Day One</u>

*Women need to reject the lie that anyone or anything can satisfy her. Only Jesus can provide the satisfaction and the joy we so desperately seek....nothing in this world can satisfy.*

1. What do you think makes a woman truly happy?

_____

_____

_____

Write out Isaiah 58:11

_____

_____

2. Do you feel that life's demand leaves you scrambling to have time set aside for God?

_____

_____

_____

Write out James 4:8

_____

_____

3. How can we make time for God a priority?

_____

_____

_____

Write out Ecclesiastes 3:1

_____

_____

4. Why is it important to make time for ourselves a priority?

_____
_____
_____

Write out Jeremiah 31:25

_____
_____

At the beginning of each week, you will rate yourself concerning three areas - where you are physically, where you are emotionally, and where you are spiritually.

Physically - 1  2  3  4  5  6  7  8  9  10

Emotionally - 1  2  3  4  5  6  7  8  9 10

Spiritually - 1  2  3  4  5  6  7  8  9  10

# Week Two - Abundant Living

<u>Day Two</u>

*Satisfaction is defined as: 1. fulfillment of one's wishes, expectations, or needs, or the pleasure derived from this. 2. the payment of a debt or fulfillment of an obligation or claim.*

1. How do you react when your wishes, expectations, or needs are not met?

_____
_____
_____

Write out  Psalm 31:15.

_____
_____

2. Do you live a life of contentment or discouragement?

_____
_____
_____

Write out  1 Samuel 30:6

_____
_____

3. Who do you turn to for trusted support when you are feeling low?

_____
_____
_____

Write out  Psalm 28:7

_____
_____

4. What do you do when you are feeling in a slump?

_____

_____

_____

Write out  Romans 8:28

_____

_____

# Week Two - Abundant Living

<u>Day Three</u>

*Life is full of days that are sunny and also some days that are stormy.*

*Stormy seasons of life are inevitable. Jesus even warned us in John 16:33 that we will have trouble in this life. He didn't leave it there though. That warning is placed between promises that He has already overcome and that He is always with us.*

1. Have you ever experienced a storm in your life?

_____

_____

_____

Write out  John 16:33

_____

_____

2. Are you experiencing a lot of pressure right now in this season of your life?

_____

_____

_____

Write out  2 Corinthians 4:8-9

_____

_____

3. How do you restore peace to high pressure circumstances in your life?

_____

_____

_____

Write out  Isaiah 26:3

_____

_____

4. Do you wait to feel a sense of peace before making decisions?

_____

_____

_____


Write out  Colossians 3:15

_____

_____

# Week Two - Abundant Living

<u>Day Four</u>

*The Abundant Life.*

1. How would you define an abundant life?

_____

_____

_____

Write out  John 10:10

_____

_____

2. Is making/having money a top priority to you?

_____

_____

_____

Write out  Matthew 19:23

_____

_____

3.  Can lack of money be a stressor for you?

_____

_____

_____

Write out  Philippians 4:6.

_____

_____

4. Can you list three things money can't buy?

_____

_____

_____

Write out  Colossians 3:2-3

_____

_____

# Week Two - Abundant Living

<u>Day Five</u>

*Going Out On A Limb.*

*For many of us, some things are worth taking the risk. It's worth buying this car even if it means eating out less for a few years. It's worth working ten hours a day so that I can send my child to college. It's worth letting go of my hobby so that I can give more time to charity work.*

1. Are you someone who will take a risk by going down a road less traveled?

_____

_____

_____

Write out Matthew 16:24-25

_____

_____

2. What are you risking your life for?

_____

_____

_____

Write out Matthew 13.44

_____

_____

3. Do you just simply let life happen to you or do you listen for the still small voice that says, "Go"?

_____

_____

_____

Write out Isaiah 30:21

_____

_____

4. Do you feel taking small steps can lead to bigger ones of faith when it comes to risk?

_____

_____

_____


Write out  Hebrews 11:6

_____

_____

# Knowing Myself

## Part One

## Week Three

## Salt & Fruit

# Week Three- Salt & Fruit

<u>Day One</u>

*Do you follow orders, recipes, or directions?*

*A definition of a follower is: 1. an adherent or devotee of a particular person, cause, or activity. 2. a person who moves or travels behind someone or something.*

1. Are there times when you are a follower?

_____

_____

Write out  Matthew 4.19

_____

_____

2. Are there times when you are a leader?

_____

_____

_____

Write out Matthew 5:13-14

_____

_____

3. Why would I want to follow someone?

_____

_____

_____

Write out  Galatians 5:22-23

_____

_____

4. Why would you stop following someone?

_____

_____

_____

Write out  Ephesians 5:11

_____

_____

At the beginning of each week, you will rate yourself concerning three areas - where you are  physically, where you are emotionally, and where you are spiritually.

Physically - 1  2  3  4  5  6  7  8  9  10

Emotionally - 1  2  3  4  5  6  7  8  9 10

Spiritually - 1  2  3  4  5  6  7  8  9  10

# Week Three - Salt & Fruit

<u>Day Two</u>

*Do I defend my beliefs?*

*Sometimes, as women, we feel we should not speak up. We don't want to be considered rude or pushy. The truth is, sharing our beliefs may be the only message about Jesus that one may hear.*

1. Have I had a time when I had to defend my beliefs?

_____

_____

_____

Write out  1 Peter 3:15

_____

_____

2. Has there been a time when I should have defended my beliefs?

_____

_____

_____

Write out  Matthew 26:72

_____

_____

3. What holds us back from defending our beliefs?

_____

_____

_____

Write out  2 Timothy 1:7

_____

_____

4. Write out at least 5 belief statements. (Belief in God, Belief that the Bible is the Word of God, etc.)

1._____

2._____

3._____

4._____

5._____

# Week Three - Salt & Fruit

<u>Day Three</u>

*Everybody has a past.*

*Sharing about our past and how giving our life to God has changed us and our behavior/circumstances is a powerful thing.*

1. Do you find yourself not sharing about your faith because of your past?

_____

_____

_____

Write out  John 4:29

_____

_____

2. Do you find things in your past a stumbling block in the present?

_____

_____

_____

Write out 2 Corinthians 5:17

_____

_____

3. Have you ever had spiritual counseling?

_____

_____

_____

Write out  James 5:16

_____

4. Why would you be hesitant to seek the counsel of a mature Christian?

_____

_____

_____

Write out  John 10:10

_____

_____

# Week Three - Salt & Fruit

<u>Day Four</u>

*Walking in the Light.*

*If we choose to neglect reading God's Word, then we will be like someone trying to walk a path at night with a flashlight filled with dead batteries. More than likely we will take a wrong turn.*

1. Is my life in alignment with the Word of God?

_____

_____

_____

Write out 1 John 1:7

_____

_____

2.  How do we know where to walk when there are so many paths to choose?

_____

_____

_____

Write out  Psalm 119:105

_____

_____

3. Can we find the right path to take on our own?

_____

_____

_____

Write out  Proverbs 3:5-6

_____

_____

4. What does reading that God has paths for you to walk mean to you?

_____

_____

_____

Write out  Psalm 23:3

_____

_____

# Week Three - Salt and Fruit

<u>Day Five</u>

*Pass the salt, please. A salty Christian makes others thirsty for Jesus.*

1. Do I have enough salt in my life?

_____

_____

_____

Write out  Mark 9:50

_____

_____

2.  Do I try to "season" where I live?

_____

_____

_____

Write out  Colossians 4:6

_____

_____

3. How would I rate my desire to be an example to others on a scale of 1 -10?   And why?

_____

_____

_____

Write out  Matthew 28:19-20

_____

_____

4. What would you want written of you in your eulogy?

_____

_____

_____

Write out  2 Timothy 4:7

_____

_____

# Knowing Myself

## Part One

## Week Four

## Honesty & Integrity

# Week Four - Honesty & Integrity

<u>Day One</u>

*Honesty - Why is it so important?*

1. Is honesty always the best policy?

_____
_____
_____

Write out Proverbs 12:22

_____
_____

2. Am I honest with others?

_____
_____
_____

Write out Ephesians 4:25

_____
_____

3. Am I honest with myself?

_____
_____
_____

Write out 1 John 1:8

_____
_____

4. Am I honest with God?

_____

_____

_____

Write out  John 4:23

_____

_____

At the beginning of each week, you will rate yourself concerning three areas - where you are physically, where you are emotionally, and where you are spiritually.

Physically - 1  2  3  4  5  6  7  8  9  10

Emotionally - 1  2  3  4  5  6  7  8  9 10

Spiritually - 1  2  3  4  5  6  7  8  9  10

# Week Four - Honesty & Integrity

<u>Day Two</u>

*As women living Christian lives in the twenty-first century, we struggle with things earlier generations never would have dreamed of. We have a balancing act of work and home life as well as connecting with people on social media. The juggle is real!*

1. Do you live your life consistently doing the right thing?

_____

_____

_____

Write out  Luke 6:31

_____

_____

2. How hard is it to live a life of integrity?

_____

_____

_____

Write out  Proverbs 21:3

_____

_____

3. Name three standards or principles that you live by.

_____

_____

_____

Write out  Proverbs 11:3

_____

_____

4. Does how I act and talk line up with being a woman of integrity?

_____

_____

_____

Write out  Psalm 101:2

_____

_____

# Week Four - Honesty

<u>Day Three</u>

*Authenticity, being the same person in public as you are in private.*

1. Do you live in such a way that your family, church, and friends know that what you say is who you are?

_____

_____

_____

Write out Proverbs 10:9

_____

_____

2. Is bending your word really that big of a deal ?

_____

_____

_____

Write out Titus 1:2

_____

_____

3. "It's not whether you win or lose, it's how you play the game." Is this phrase true?

_____

_____

_____

Write out 1 Peter 3:16

_____

_____

4. How could walking in integrity be like a shield for us?

_____

_____

_____

Write out  Psalm 26:11

_____

_____

# Week Four - Honesty & Integrity

<u>Day Four</u>

*Integrity isn't something that only the very righteous can obtain. Integrity is available to all of us. Integrity is a choice; a choice to continue making the right choices.*

1. Would following a list of Dos and Don'ts make it easier to know what is the right thing to always do?

_____
_____
_____

Write out  James 1:5

_____
_____

2. Describe how acting with integrity would align with your beliefs.

_____
_____
_____

Write out  James 1:25

_____
_____

3. What is a reason that a person might be tempted to not be honest?

_____
_____
_____

Write out  Psalm 101:7

_____
_____

4. We don't want anything to hinder our relationship with God and with others. How could not practicing honesty affect our relationships, our testimony, and our eternity?

_____

_____

_____

Write out  2 Corinthians 8:21

_____

_____

# Week Four - Honesty & Integrity

<u>Day Five</u>

*Money isn't evil. How we feel about money and how we act about getting and keeping money is what can become an issue. Money is a tool and one we need to use wisely.*

_____
_____
_____

Write out 1 Timothy 6:10

_____
_____

2. Can money bring us happiness?

_____
_____
_____

Write out Hebrews 13:5

_____
_____

3. Is it wrong to want to have the nicer things in life?

_____
_____
_____

Write out Luke 12:15

_____
_____

4. Do you watch your spending?

_____

_____

_____

Write out  Proverbs 13:11

_____

_____

# Knowing Myself

## Part One

## Week Five

## Financially Smart

# Week Five - Financially Smart

<u>Day One</u>

*Our finances are an important aspect of our lives, which means we have to understand and manage them well.*

1. Do you budget the money you have?

_____

_____

_____

Write out  Ecclesiastes 5.10

_____

_____

2. Do you feel that you have a healthy relationship with money?

_____

_____

_____

Write out  Luke 16:13

_____

_____

3.  Do you stop to consider the financial implication of a decision before anything else?

_____

_____

_____

Write out  Proverbs 21:5

_____

_____

4. Do you have a "trigger" that makes you want to spend money?

_____

_____

_____

Write out  Ezekiel 7:19

_____

_____

At the beginning of each week, you will rate yourself concerning these areas – where you are physically, where you are emotionally, and where you are spiritually.

Physically-  1  2  3  4  5  6  7  8  9  10

Emotionally- 1  2  3  4  5  6  7  8  9  10

Spiritually-  1  2  3  4  5  6  7  8  9  10

# Week Five - Financially Smart

<u>Day Two</u>

*Earnings*

1. Is it okay to expect income from what we do?

_____

_____

_____

Write out  1 Timothy 5:18

_____

_____

2. Why shouldn't our focus be on earning money for money's sake?

_____

_____

_____

Write out Proverbs 22:1

_____

_____

3. Is it okay to expect income from what we do even if it is for the kingdom of God?

_____

_____

_____

Write out  1 Timothy 5:17

_____

_____

4. Do you think people who put their money toward a purpose are better able to meet their goals?

_____

_____

_____

Write out  Luke 14:28

_____

_____

# Week Five - Financially Smart

<u>Day Three</u>

*Everything comes from God.*

1. What happens when we realize that everything comes from God?

_____

_____

_____

Write out  1 Chronicles 29:16

_____

_____

2. Do you tithe?

_____

_____

_____

Write out  Malachi 3:10

_____

_____

3. How are tithing and giving different?

_____

_____

Write out  Proverbs 11:25

_____

_____

4. Do we use what we have been given to glorify God?

_____

_____

_____

Write out  Matthew 25:21

_____

_____

# Week Five - Financially Smart

<u>Day Four</u>

*Financial awareness and financial education are key.*

*Preparing for the future does not mean a lack of faith but a sign of wisdom.*

1. Have you thought about steps you can take to become better prepared for the years to come?

_____

_____

_____

Write out  Proverbs 6:6

_____

_____

2. Why is women's financial struggles with making ends meet often a taboo subject?

_____

_____

_____

Write out Proverbs 11:28

_____

_____

3. Do you take charge of your financial future or leave it in the hands of another?

_____

_____

_____

Write out  Proverbs 31:17-18

_____

_____

4. What steps could you take to become more proactive concerning your finances?

_____

_____

_____

Write out  Proverbs 31:21

_____

_____

53

# Week Five - Financially Smart

<u>Day Five</u>

1. How is your credit score?

_____

_____

_____

Write out  Ecclesiastes 7:1

_____

_____

2. Have you considered having life insurance?

_____

_____

_____

Write out  Proverbs 27:12

_____

_____

3. Do you know how much you will need to live in retirement?

_____

_____

_____

Write out  Jeremiah 29:11

_____

_____

4. How does knowing that God has planned for our welfare and not our calamity make you feel about our future finances?

_____

_____

_____

Write out  James 1:17

_____

_____

# Knowing Myself

# Part One

## Week Six

## Being Genuine

# Week Six – Being Genuine

<u>Day One</u>

*We live in a time when people have many different thoughts on many subjects.*

1. Do we know that not everyone thinks like we do?

_____

_____

_____

Write out  Romans 14:1-2

_____

_____

2. How does having different life experiences shape how we think?

_____

_____

_____

Write out  Job 12:12

_____

_____

3. Are we dismissive of others who don't agree with what we think?

_____

_____

_____

Write out  Ephesians 4:1-2

_____

_____

4. Why does it take work to understand someone's point of view?

_____

_____

_____

Write out  Hebrews 12:14

_____

_____

At the beginning of every week, you will rate yourself concerning three areas – where you are physically, where you are emotionally, and where you are spiritually.

Physically -  1  2  3  4  5  6  7  8  9  10

Emotionally -  1  2  3  4  5  6  7  8  9  10

Spiritually -  1  2  3  4  5  6  7  8  9  10

# Week Six - Being Genuine

<u>Day Two</u>

*We live in a Society that puts great emphasis on "being authentic."*

1. Society wants us to tell it like it is. Would being truthful with someone without being brutally honest challenge our "authentic self"?

_____

_____

_____

Write out  Ephesians 4:15

_____

_____

2. Do you think people could feel they have license to say hurtful and destructive things because of a misunderstanding of what being authentic means?

_____

_____

_____

Write out  1 Corinthians 13:11

_____

_____

3. Would you say being authentic is more about what you say than what you do?

_____

_____

_____

Write out James 1:19

_____

_____

4. How do we live our lives authentically?

_____

_____

_____

Write out  Luke 9:23

_____

_____

# Week Six - Being Genuine

Day Three

*We are living in an age of identity crisis. You choose who you want to be today and change your mind tomorrow, taking on a new identity.*

1. Do you ever ask yourself, "Who am I?"

_____

_____

_____

Write out  Galatians 3:26-28

_____

_____

2. How can what others say to us or about us impact how we see ourselves?

_____

_____

_____

Write out  Matthew 11:28

_____

_____

3. Have you ever allowed someone to cause you to feel ineffective, inadequate?

_____

_____

_____

Write out  2 Corinthians 12:9

_____

_____

4. How does knowing the truth give you the freedom to just be you?

_____

Write out  Job 33:4

# Week Six - Being Genuine

<u>Day Four</u>

*Being genuine doesn't mean being judgmental.*

1. Are you at times judgmental of others who don't adhere to the same convictions as you?

_____

_____

_____

Write out  Matthew 7:1-2

_____

_____

2. Are women often quick to criticize and judge other women?

_____

_____

_____

Write out  1 Peter 5:5

_____

_____

3. Why is it hard to live in a society where the World and Christians can shout, "Don't judge me!"?

_____

_____

_____

Write out  Galatians 6:1-2

_____

_____

4. How can concern for others when they are getting off track be defined as being genuine?

_____

_____

_____

Write out  Matthew 18:15

_____

_____

# Week Six – Being Genuine

<u>Day Five</u>

*As women, we're not on a mission to be Super Woman, but rather a woman who is empowered by our faith in God.*

1. Do you ever feel as though others expect you to be Super Woman?

_____

_____

_____

Write out  Proverbs 31: 17, 25

_____

_____

2. Is there an area of your life where you feel powerless?

_____

_____

_____

Write out  1 Peter 3:6

_____

_____

3. How can acting like "I've got this" and  "I can handle it" be a negative in the long run?

_____

_____

_____

Write out  John 15:5

_____

_____

4. At times, could the pressure we feel to be like Super Woman be self-induced?

_____

_____

_____

Write out  James 1:13

_____

_____

# Learning

## Part Two

## Week One

## Actions Become Habits

# Week One - Actions Become Habits

<u>Day One</u>

*Have you ever heard the saying, "Sow a thought, reap an action. Sow an action, reap a habit. Sow a habit, reap a character. Sow a character, reap a destiny!"*

1. How can what we think about be a directive for our lives?

_____

_____

_____

Write out  Proverbs 23:7

_____

_____

2. What is a way that you could take control of what you think about?

_____

_____

_____

Write out  Philippians 4:8

_____

_____

3. Have you ever had someone say something negative to you that you could not stop replaying in your mind?

_____

_____

_____

Write out  2 Corinthians 10:5

_____

_____

4. Author, Joyce Meyer, has been quoted as saying that, "Too many people have 'Stinkin Thinkin'." Are there areas of your thought life that you need to take control of?

_____

_____

_____

Write out  2 Corinthians 10:4

_____

_____

_____

At the beginning of each week, you will rate yourself concerning these areas – where you are physically, where you are emotionally, and where you are spiritually.

Physically-  1  2  3  4  5  6  7  8  9  10

Emotionally- 1  2  3  4  5  6  7  8  9  10

Spiritually-  1  2  3  4  5  6  7  8  9  10

# Week One - Actions Become Habits

<u>Day Two</u>

*We all have habits, some good, some bad. Habits can form early. A baby's natural rooting reflex can have them starting to suck their thumbs before they are even born!*

1. Could our habits reveal what is truly important to us?

_____

_____

_____

Write out 1 Corinthians 11:1

_____

_____

2. How could the practice of our habits shape us in the days to come?

_____

_____

_____

Write out Colossians 2:8

_____

_____

3. Can you name some habits that would be beneficial to incorporate into our daily lives?

_____

_____

_____

Write out  1 Thessalonians 5:16-18

_____

_____

4. Why should spending time with God be our number one habit?

_____

_____

_____

Write out  Proverbs 3:6

_____

_____

# Week One - Actions Become Habits

<u>Day Three</u>

*The first step to removing bad habits from our lives is to make an honest assessment of them.*

1. How might we purge bad habits from our lives?

_____

_____

_____

Write out  Proverbs 28:13

_____

_____

2. Why are bad habits so easy to point out in others and just as easy to ignore in ourselves?

_____

_____

_____

Write out Matthew 7:3

_____

_____

3. Could someone have a bad habit in their life that they could never be rid of?

_____

_____

_____

Write out Romans 8:31

_____

_____

4. Could grumbling and complaining become a habit?

_____

_____

_____

Write out  Philippians 2:14-15

_____

_____

# Week One - Actions Become Habits

<u>Day Four</u>

*We are a spirit, possessing a soul, housed in a body. It is only natural that we have habits relating to each.*

1. How important is it that we cultivate good habits for our physical health?

_____

_____

_____

Write out 1 Corinthians 6:19-20

_____

_____

2. Do you implement the habit of exercise in your weekly routine?

_____

_____

_____

Write out 1 Corinthians 9:26-27

_____

_____

3. Why is it hard to be motivated in the area of physical fitness?

_____

_____

_____

Write out  1 Timothy 4:8

_____

_____

4. Are you aware of the recommended exercise for your age group?

_____

_____

_____

Write out  2 Corinthians 4:16

_____

_____

# Week One - Actions Become Habits

<u>Day Five</u>

1. Why is nourishing our spirits, souls, and bodies so important?

_____

_____

_____

Write Matthew 11:28-29

_____

_____

2. Do you ever feel like you are running on empty?

_____

_____

_____

Write out John 7:38

_____

_____

3. Do you drink enough water?

_____

_____

_____

Write out John 4:14

_____

_____

4. Do you eat a balanced diet?

_____

Write out  Matthew 4:4

# Learning

## Part Two

## Week Two

## Being Sensitive to Others

# Week Two - Being Sensitive to Others

Day One

*Listening is key to effective communicating.*

1. Are you a good listener?

_____

_____

_____

Write out Proverbs 18:13

_____

_____

2. Have you ever had someone "half-listen" to you?

_____

_____

_____

Write out Proverbs 18:2

_____

_____

3. Do you think that hearing could be different than listening?

_____

_____

_____

Write out John 13:34

_____

_____

4. How could miscommunication and misunderstandings arise over not truly listening?

_____

_____

_____

Write out  Colossians 3:13

_____

_____

At the beginning of each week, you will rate yourself concerning these areas – where you are physically, where you are emotionally, and where you are spiritually.

Physically- 1  2  3  4  5  6  7  8  9  10

Emotionally- 1  2  3  4  5  6  7  8  9  10

Spiritually- 1  2  3  4  5  6  7  8  9  10

# Week Two - Being Sensitive to Others

<u>Day Two</u>

1. How important is it to try and get along with others who may disregard how we feel about things?

_____
_____
_____

Write out  Romans 12:18

_____
_____

2. How sensitive do we remain to people who have totally different views and opinions than us?

_____
_____
_____

Write out  Acts 15:39

_____
_____

3. How would you handle a situation where a person is always disrespectful concerning your feelings and beliefs?

_____
_____
_____

Write out  Romans 12:14

_____
_____

4. What is a way that sensitivity could be maintained, and communication continue between people who have differing views?

_____

_____

_____

Write out  Matthew 22:37-39

_____

_____

# Week Two - Being Sensitive to Others

<u>Day Three</u>

*How can we make an impact where we live?*

1. Do you know those who live in the homes near you?

_____

_____

_____

Write out  Philippians 2:4

_____

_____

2. Do you believe that where you live is by coincidence?

_____

_____

_____

Write out  Acts 17:26

_____

_____

3. How could you be intentional about following Jesus' command to love your neighbor?

_____

_____

_____

Write out  1 Corinthians 10:24

_____

_____

4. Since scripture about loving our neighbor is found in the Bible eight times do you think this would be

something we should strive to do?

_____

_____

_____

Write out  Matthew 5:16

_____

_____

# Week Two - Being Sensitive to Others

<u>Day Four</u>

*Maintaining sensitivity with people who are critical.*

1. How can we handle overly critical people in our lives?

_____

_____

_____

Write out  Luke 17:1

_____

_____

2. How can we arm ourselves against criticism from people?

_____

_____

_____

Write out  Philippians 4:13

_____

_____

3. Do you think some people feel they have free reign to be critical with people of faith?

_____

_____

_____

Write out 1 Corinthians 16:13

_____

_____

4. Why can the words of a critic hurt?

---

---

---

Write out  Luke 6:27-28

---

---

# Week One - Being Sensitive to Others

<u>Day Five</u>

*How do we speak to people?*

1. Do the words we say to others really matter?

_____

_____

_____

Write out  Proverbs 15:1

_____

_____

2. Have you ever experienced a time when someone's words hurt you?

_____

_____

_____

Write out  Proverbs 15:4

_____

_____

3. What impact do you wish your words to have on others?

_____

_____

_____

Write out  Ephesians 4:29

_____

_____

4. How do we know the right thing to say to those who may be having a difficult time?

_____

_____

_____

Write out  Proverbs 16:24

_____

_____

# Learning

## Part Two

## Week Three

## Seasons

# Week Three - Seasons

<u>Day One</u>

*Friends through the seasons of life*

1. Have you built true friendships?

_____

_____

_____

Write out  Ruth 1:16

_____

_____

2. What words would you use to describe a true friendship?

_____

_____

_____

Write out  Ecclesiastes 4:9

_____

3. What can friends teach us about ourselves?

_____

_____

_____

Write out  Proverbs 27:9

_____

_____

4. How could a true friend strengthen you?

_____

_____

_____

Write out  Psalms 18:39

_____

_____

At the beginning of each week, you will rate yourself concerning these areas – where you are physically, where you are emotionally, and where you are spiritually.

Physically- 1  2  3  4  5  6  7  8  9  10

Emotionally- 1  2  3  4  5  6  7  8  9  10

Spiritually- 1  2  3  4  5  6  7  8  9  10

# Week Three - Seasons

<u>Day Two</u>

*Seasons of Change.*

1. How well do you handle change?

_____

_____

_____

Write out  Philippians 4:11

_____

_____

2. Could facing changes challenge us to trust God in new ways as we put our faith in Him?

_____

_____

_____

Write out  Isaiah 43:19

_____

_____

3. If we know change is inevitable what steps could we take to learn to embrace it rather than try to deflect it?

_____

_____

_____

Write out  2 Corinthians 9:8

_____

_____

4. Can you change without growing?

_____

_____

_____

Write out  Galatians 6:9

_____

_____

# Week Three - Seasons

<u>Day Three</u>

*The seasons of change.*

1. We are all in different seasons of our lives. It may be a dry season, an abundant season, a waiting season, or something else. What are some of the challenges of the season of life you are in right now?

_____

_____

_____

Write out  Daniel 2:21

_____

_____

2. What perspective helps you get through a season?

_____

_____

_____

Write out  Psalms 74:17

_____

_____

3. Are you someone who can wait patiently?

_____

_____

_____

Write out  Psalm 37:7

_____

_____

4. Do you ever feel like God has forgotten that you are sitting in the Waiting Room?

_____

_____

_____

Write out  Psalm 5:3

_____

_____

# Week Three - Seasons

<u>Day Four</u>

*Pursuing patience.*

*Patience - the capacity to accept or tolerate delay, trouble, or suffering without getting angry or upset.*

1. Is the definition of patience, and the way you practice being patient, in alignment with one another?

_____

_____

_____

Write out  1 Timothy 6:11

_____

_____

2. How can we choose to be patient through delay, trouble, or suffering?

_____

_____

_____

Write out  Colossians 3:20

_____

_____

3. What could be a benefit of being patient?

_____

_____

_____

Write out  Hebrews 6:15

_____

_____

4. Can we fake patience?

_____

_____

_____

Write out Romans 15:5

_____

_____

# Week Three - Seasons

<u>Day Five</u>

*Patience Role Models.*

1. List three people in your life that have been patient with you.

_____

_____

_____

2. What defined their patience?

_____

_____

_____

Write out  Corinthians 13:4

_____

_____

3. How could modeling patience influence others?

_____

_____

_____

Write out  Colossians 1:11

_____

_____

4. What enables a person to remain patient?

_____

_____

_____

Write out  2 Thessalonians 3:5

_____

_____

# Learning

## Part Two

## Week Four

## Focusing Our Hearts

# Week Four - Growing in Grace

<u>Day One</u>

*Focusing our Hearts.*

*Women today can feel pressured to be perfect.*

1. Do women today strive for perfection?

_____

_____

_____

Write out  2 Corinthians 13:11

_____

_____

2. How realistic is perfection?

_____

_____

_____

Write out  Philippians 3:12

_____

_____

3. If you are a woman who strives for perfection, what is your motivation?

_____

_____

_____

Write out  Colossians 3:1

_____

_____

4. Can you strive for perfection even if struggling with brokenness and everyday challenges?

_____

_____

_____

Write out 2 Corinthians 12:9

_____

_____

At the beginning of each week, you will rate yourself concerning these areas – where you are physically, where you are emotionally, and where you are spiritually.

Physically- 1 2 3 4 5 6 7 8 9 10

Emotionally- 1 2 3 4 5 6 7 8 9 10

Spiritually- 1 2 3 4 5 6 7 8 9 10

# Week Four - Growing in Grace

<u>Day Two</u>

*Divine Grace.*

*Oswald Chambers wrote, "Beware of looking back at what you once were, when God wants you to become someone you've never been."*

1. Have you ever experienced a setback or a failure?

_____
_____
_____

Write out  2 Corinthians 3:18

_____
_____

2. What happens when we focus only on our failures?

_____
_____
_____

Write out  Ephesians 2:10

_____
_____

3. How might God use a failure?

_____
_____
_____

Write out  Romans 3:24

_____
_____

4. Has anyone ever said words to you that made you feel like a failure?

_____

_____

_____

Write out  2 Corinthians 5:17

_____

_____

# Week Four - Growing in Grace

<u>Day Three</u>

*Handling conflict.*

1. When people say or do mean or hurtful things to us, what is our first gut reaction?

_____

_____

_____

Write out  Matthew 5:38-39

_____

_____

2. How well do you handle conflict?

_____

_____

_____

Write out  Psalm 133:1

_____

_____

3. How can conflict ruin relationships?

_____

_____

_____

Write out  Matthew 5:9

_____

_____

4. Could a conflict be resolved even if two people can't come to an agreement?

---
---
---

Write out  2 Corinthians 6:3

---
---

# Week Four - Growing in Grace

<u>Day Four</u>

*Handling conflict.*

1. What steps do you take to resolve a conflict?

_____
_____
_____

Write out  Luke 17:3

_____
_____

2. How can we be cooperative in overcoming conflict?

_____
_____
_____

Write out  Hebrews 12:15

_____
_____

3. Why is it important that we not gossip about conflict?

_____
_____
_____

Write out  Philippians 2:3

_____
_____

4. What do you do if every avenue of working to resolve a conflict doesn't work?

_____

_____

_____

Write out  Romans 12:17-18

_____

_____

# Week Four - Growing in Grace

<u>Day Five</u>

*Gossip-Go-Round.*

*We live in a culture of gossip, and everything seems fair game.*

1. How would you define gossip?

_____

_____

_____

Write out  Proverbs 16:28

_____

_____

2. How do you handle gossip?

_____

_____

_____

Write out  Matthew 15:18

_____

_____

3. Why do we fall into gossiping?

_____

_____

_____

Write out  Romans 1:28-30

_____

_____

4. What steps could someone take to squelch gossip?

_____

_____

_____

Write out  Proverbs 21:23

_____

_____

# Learning

## Part Two

## Week Five

## R.E.S.P.E.C.T.

# Week Five - R.E.S.P.E.C.T.

<u>Day One</u>

*Being Respectful.*

*Respect is a way of treating or thinking about something or someone.*

1.  Do you think there is a lack of respect in the world today?

_____

_____

_____

Write out  1 Peter 2:17

_____

_____

2. How do we show respect to others?

_____

_____

_____

Write out  Romans 12:10

_____

_____

3. Can you be respectful without being humble?

_____

_____

_____

Write out  Matthew 23:12

_____

_____

4. What might keep a person from being respectful?

_____

_____

_____

Write out  Isaiah 2:12

_____

_____

At the beginning of each week, you will rate yourself concerning these areas – where you are physically, where you are emotionally, and where you are spiritually.

Physically-  1  2  3  4  5  6  7  8  9  10

Emotionally- 1  2  3  4  5  6  7  8  9  10

Spiritually-  1  2  3  4  5  6  7  8  9  10

# Week Five - R.E.S.P.E.C.T.

<u>Day Two</u>

*Examples of respect.*

1. Write down two people you consider to be respectful.

_____

_____

_____

2. Why would you say they are respectful?

_____

_____

_____

3. What lessons have they taught you?

_____

_____

_____

Write out  Matthew 7:12

_____

_____

4. Name something that would surprise you if you saw one of the above-mentioned people do.

_____

_____

Write out  Mark 9:42

_____

_____

# Week Five - R.E.S.P.E.C.T.

<u>Day Three</u>

*Being respectful.*

1. How can we be respectful to our family?

_____

_____

_____

Write out  1 Timothy 5:8

_____

_____

2. How could a woman show respect to her husband?

_____

_____

_____

Write out  Titus 2:4-5

_____

_____

3. Why is it important that children be respectful to their parents?

_____

_____

_____

Write out  Exodus 20:12

_____

_____

4. Why is praying for our future husband, or the one we have been married to 5, 10, 25, 45 or more years

be a way to respect them?

_____

_____

_____

Write out  Proverbs 14:1

_____

_____

# Week Five - R.E.S.P.E.C.T.

<u>Day Four</u>

*Respect on the job.*

1. How can we be a respectful coworker?

_____

_____

_____

Write out  Titus 2:7

_____

_____

2. How could we show sensitivity in the workplace?

_____

_____

_____

Write out  Colossians 3:23-24

_____

_____

3. How easy is it to be respectful when others are not?

_____

_____

_____

Write out  Matthew 5:44

_____

_____

4. How can understanding why a person acts disrespectfully help us in dealing with them?

_____

_____

_____

Write out Proverbs 21:2

_____

_____

# Week Five - R.E.S.P.E.C.T.

<u>Day Five</u>

*Ways we show respect.*

1. What does it say when a person is punctual?

_____

_____

_____

Write out  John 7:6

_____

_____

2.  How could giving someone a compliment be a show of respect?

_____

_____

_____

Write out  Proverbs 12:25

_____

_____

3. How well do you receive a compliment?

_____

_____

_____

Write out  1 Thessalonians 5:11

_____

_____

4. Why is it important to do what you say?

_____

_____

_____

Write out  Matthew 5:37

_____

_____

# Learning

## Part Two

## Week Six

## Works in Progress

# Week Six - Works in Progress

<u>Day One</u>

*Focusing on forgiveness.*

1. Is there anything unresolved in our families, current or past?

_____

_____

_____

Write out  Philippians 3:13

_____

_____

2. How can we forgive those who should never have hurt us?

_____

_____

_____

Write out  Matthew 18:21-22

_____

_____

3. Could we sentence ourselves over something?

_____

_____

_____

Write out  1 John 1:9

_____

_____

4. What happens when we offer and/or receive forgiveness?

_____

_____

_____

Write out  Matthew 5:23-24

_____

_____

# Week Six - Works in Progress

<u>Day Two</u>

*God's desire is for us to grow closer to Him and to witness to those we come in contact with.*

1.  Are we aware that we have a purpose?

_____
_____
_____

Write out  Isaiah 64:8

_____
_____

2.  Does our purpose have an expiration date?

_____
_____
_____

Write out  Luke 2:36-37

_____
_____

3. Can our marriage put our purpose on hold?

_____
_____
_____

Write out  1 Peter 3:1-2

_____
_____

4. Can our singleness cancel our purpose?

_____

_____

_____

Write out  Isaiah 54:5

_____

_____

# Week Six - Works in Progress

<u>Day Three</u>

*Worry.*

*The definition of worry is - give way to anxiety or unease, allow one's mind to dwell on difficulty or troubles.*

1. What causes someone to worry?

_____

_____

_____

Write out  Matthew 6:25

_____

_____

2. How does someone tackle worry?

_____

_____

_____

Write out  Matthew 6:34

_____

_____

3. How can worry steal our peace?

_____

_____

_____

Write out  Matthew 6:27

_____

_____

4. How could making a plan against worry help us rise above its temptation?

_____

_____

_____

Write out  Isaiah 41:10

_____

_____

# Week Six - Works in Progress

<u>Day Four</u>

*Being honest about where we are.*

1. What would you say are your personal strengths?

_____

_____

_____

Write out  2 Peter 1:10

_____

_____

2. What would you say are your personal weaknesses?

_____

_____

_____

Write out  Lamentations 3:40

_____

_____

3. Are you open to improvement?

_____

_____

_____

Write out  Psalm 119:59

_____

_____

4. How could allowing others to see our weaknesses be productive?

_____

_____

_____

Write out  2 Corinthians 12:10

_____

_____

# Week Six - Works in Progress

<u>Day Five</u>

*Accepting where we are.*

1. What do we need to accept about our lives?

_____

_____

_____

Write out  Galatians 6:4

_____

_____

2. How do we feel when we are following God, but things are not turning out like we had planned?

_____

_____

_____

Write out  Psalm 16:11

_____

_____

3. How can we remain hopeful in the midst of unanswered prayer?

_____

_____

_____

Write out  Habakkuk 3:17-18

_____

_____

4. What in our lives is a cause for celebration?

_____

_____

_____

Write out  Romans 5:5

_____

_____

# Leading

## Part Three

## Week One

## Leading as a Role Model

# Week One - Leading

<u>Day One</u>

*Defining a leader.*

1. What defines a leader?

_____

_____

_____

Write out  Hebrews 13:17

_____

_____

2. If leadership is defined as influence then what does that mean to us in our lives?

_____

_____

_____

Write out  Romans 12:8

_____

_____

3. Can we be faithful leaders even if we are not the one "in charge"?

_____

_____

_____

Write out  2 Timothy 2:15

_____

_____

4. How could being cooperative and following our leaders prepare us to lead?

_____

_____

_____

Write out Hebrews 13:7

_____

_____

At the beginning of each week, you will rate yourself concerning these areas – where you are physically, where you are emotionally, and where you are spiritually.

Physically- 1  2  3  4  5  6  7  8  9  10

Emotionally- 1  2  3  4  5  6  7  8  9  10

Spiritually- 1  2  3  4  5  6  7  8  9  10

# Week One - Leading

<u>Day Two</u>

*Defining a role model.*

1. How would you define a role model?

_____

_____

_____

Write out Proverbs 22:1

_____

_____

2. How easily are some people influenced?

_____

_____

_____

Write out Proverbs 13:20

_____

_____

3. Why do people want role models?

_____

_____

_____

Write out Psalm 1:1-3

_____

_____

4. Why do people need role models?

_____

_____

_____

Write out  Isaiah 26:7

_____

_____

# Week One - Leading

<u>Day Three</u>

*Who has been, or is currently, our role models?*

1. Write down two role models in our life.

_____

_____

_____

Write out  Philippians 3:17

_____

_____

2. What kind of attitudes do our role models have?

_____

_____

_____

Write out  Philippians 2:5

_____

_____

3. Other than their attitudes, why do we see them as role models?

_____

_____

_____

Write out  1 John 2:6

_____

_____

4. What lessons have we been taught by our role models?

_____

_____

_____

Write out  John 13:15

_____

_____

# Week One - Leading

<u>Day Four</u>

*How can we inspire others as a role model?*

1. How do you feel about being someone's role model?

_____

_____

_____

Write out Hebrews 6:11

_____

_____

2. How does our attitude affect others?

_____

_____

_____

Write out Jonah 4:9

_____

_____

3. Who is someone in your life that you have some influence over?

_____

_____

_____

Write out 2 Thessalonians 3:7

_____

_____

4. Who in your life would you like to be a Godly role model to?

_____

_____

_____

Write out  2 Thessalonians 5:22

_____

_____

# Week One - Leading

<u>Day Five</u>

*What happens when there is a bad role model?*

1. What are two ways that a person can be a bad role model?

_____

_____

_____

Write out  Romans 2:24

_____

_____

2. How can a negative role model lead people astray?

_____

_____

_____

Write out  1 Corinthians 8:9

_____

_____

3. How does a negative role model break trust?

_____

_____

_____

Write out  1 Samuel 19:6

_____

_____

4. How much influence do role models have?

Write out  Numbers 16:3

# Leading

## Part Three

## Week Two

## Being a Follower

# Week Two - Leading

<u>Day One</u>

*Everyone follows someone or something.*

1. Who have we followed?

_____

_____

_____

Write out  Matthew 16:24

_____

_____

2. Why did we follow them?

_____

_____

_____

Write out  John 8:2

_____

_____

3. What do you think about the fact that others may be following us?

_____

_____

_____

Write out Titus 2:3-5

_____

_____

4. Why do women need relationships with other women?

_____

_____

_____

Write out  Ecclesiastes 4:9

_____

_____

At the beginning of each week, you will rate yourself concerning these areas – where you are physically, where you are emotionally, and where you are spiritually.

Physically-  1  2  3  4  5  6  7  8  9  10

Emotionally- 1  2  3  4  5  6  7  8  9  10

Spiritually-  1  2  3  4  5  6  7  8  9  10

# Week Two - Leading

<u>Day Two</u>

*Why we need to follow.*

1. How does following someone encourage us to personally grow?

_____

_____

_____

Write out Matthew 4:20

_____

_____

2. How willing are we to be taught?

_____

_____

_____

Write out 1 Peter 2:21

_____

_____

3. How can we honor someone's wisdom?

_____

_____

_____

Write out Matthew 24:35

_____

_____

4. Can we follow someone who is no longer alive?

Write out  Hebrews 11:2

# Week Two - Leading

<u>Day Three</u>

*How to be a good follower.*

1. Are we willing to follow?

_____

_____

_____

Write out  Galatians 5:25

_____

_____

2. Do we tend to see the negative or the positive?

_____

_____

_____

Write out  John 6:68

_____

_____

3. How do you recognize the trustworthiness of someone you are following?

_____

_____

_____

Write out  Proverbs 11:13

_____

_____

4. What lesson has been pointed out to you that you had not thought about?

Write out  John 9:3

# Week Two - Leading

<u>Day Four</u>

*Being a bad follower.*

1. How would not listening affect our following?

_____

_____

_____

Write out  John 10:27

_____

_____

2. Do we really know that we have more to learn?

_____

_____

_____

Write out  Mark 10:21

_____

_____

3. A bad follower second guesses who she is following. Have we been guilty of second guessing?

_____

_____

_____

Write out  Matthew 8:22

_____

_____

4. A bad follower may betray the person they are following. Why would that be bad?

Write out  Luke 22:4

# Week Two - Leading

<u>Day Five</u>

*A good leader always begins as a good follower.*

1. Do we enjoy following?

_____

_____

_____

Write out  Psalm 55:22

_____

_____

2. How can we encourage others to follow?

_____

_____

_____

Write out  John 6:2

_____

_____

3. How can we honor those we are following?

_____

_____

_____

Write out  Psalm 1:1

_____

_____

4. How can we follow the example of the mentors in our lives?

_____

_____

_____

Write out  1 Corinthians 11:2

_____

_____

# Leading

## Part Three

## Week Three

## Being Hopeful

# Week Three - Leading

<u>Day One</u>

*What does it mean to be hopeful?*

1. How can we see good when there is a lot of bad around?

_____

_____

_____

Write out  Philippians 4:19

_____

_____

2. When we are having problems, how can we know that better days are coming?

_____

_____

_____

Write out  Revelation 22:20

_____

_____

3. Do we know that our troubles won't last forever?

_____

_____

_____

Write out  Proverbs 29:25

_____

_____

4. How can we know we will get through the tough times?

_____

_____

_____

Write out  Romans 8:18

_____

_____

At the beginning of each week, you will rate yourself concerning these areas – where you are physically, where you are emotionally, and where you are spiritually.

Physically-  1  2  3  4  5  6  7  8  9  10

Emotionally- 1  2  3  4  5  6  7  8  9  10

Spiritually-  1  2  3  4  5  6  7  8  9  10

# Week Three - Leading

<u>Day Two</u>

*The world needs hope.*

1. How easy is it to find bad news?

_____

_____

_____

Write out  Job 1:16

_____

_____

2. Do you think it is true that many people are negative?

_____

_____

_____

Write out  Nehemiah 4:1

_____

_____

3. How discouraging can it be when it seems we are always facing challenges?

_____

_____

_____

Write out  Psalm 9:9

_____

_____

4. How fast does bad news spread?

_____

_____

_____

Write out  Psalm 55:6-8

_____

_____

# Week Three - Leading

<u>Day Three</u>

*Who has been hopeful in our life?*

1. List two people who you would describe as being hopeful.

_____

_____

_____

2. Why do you say they are hopeful?

_____

_____

_____

3. What two lessons have you learned from their lives?

_____

_____

_____

4. How can we be more like them?

_____

_____

_____

Write out 1 Thessalonians 1:3

_____

_____

# Week Three - Leading

<u>Day Four</u>

*What happens if someone is not hopeful?*

1. Do people want to be around someone who is disparaging?

_____

_____

_____

Write out  Proverbs 24:1

_____

_____

2. How can someone not being hopeful miss out on something?

_____

_____

_____

Write out  Romans 8:35

_____

_____

3. How can those who are not hopeful discourage others?

_____

_____

_____

Write out  Numbers 13:32

_____

_____

4. How can being hopeful help us deal with stress?

_____

_____

_____

Write out  Proverbs 17:22

_____

_____

# Week Three - Leading

<u>Day Five</u>

*Benefits of being hopeful.*

1. How can being hopeful encourage us?

_____

_____

_____

Write out  Psalm 23:4

_____

_____

2. How can being hopeful help us to see the big picture?

_____

_____

_____

Write out  Matthew 16:16

_____

_____

3. How can being hopeful impact our health?

_____

_____

_____

Write out  Psalm 147:3

_____

_____

4. How can someone who is not hopeful depress us?

_____

_____

_____

Write out  Exodus 16:2

_____

_____

# Leading

## Part Three

## Week Four

## Being Humble

# Week Four - Leading

<u>Day One</u>

*What does it mean to be humble?*

1. Is it easy to accept our limitations?

_____
_____
_____

Write out  Proverbs 16:18

_____
_____

2. How can being grateful help us to be humble?

_____
_____
_____

Write out  Ephesians 2:8-9

_____
_____

3. How easy is it to admit we make mistakes?

_____
_____
_____

Write out  2 Chronicles 7:14

_____
_____

4. How can being humble help us avoid bragging?

_____

_____

_____

Write out 1 Peter 5:6

_____

_____

At the beginning of each week, you will rate yourself concerning these areas – where you are physically, where you are emotionally, and where you are spiritually.

Physically- 1 2 3 4 5 6 7 8 9 10

Emotionally- 1 2 3 4 5 6 7 8 9 10

Spiritually- 1 2 3 4 5 6 7 8 9 10

# Week Four - Leading

<u>Day Two</u>

*People we know who are humble.*

1. List two people who you think are humble.

_____

_____

2. Why do you say they are humble?

_____

_____

_____

3. How does their humbleness affect you?

_____

_____

_____

Write out Proverbs 11:2

_____

_____

4. Do we reflect on areas where we can be more humble?

_____

_____

Write out Ephesians 4:2

_____

_____

# Week Four - Leading

<u>Day Three</u>

*The effects of not being humble.*

1. Can a person be humble if they don't recognize their faults?

_____

_____

_____

Write out  Matthew 23:12

_____

_____

2. How does being humble help us not to be afraid of making mistakes?

_____

_____

_____

Write out  Jeremiah 17:9

_____

_____

3. Do humble persons compare themselves to others?

_____

_____

_____

Write out  Luke 18:11

_____

_____

4. Does a humble person seek the limelight?

_____

_____

_____

Write out  Proverbs 27:2

_____

_____

# Week Four - Leading

<u>Day Four</u>

*How humility affects others.*

1. How does being humble help us to be considerate in our conversations with others?

_____

_____

_____

Write out  Colossians 4:6

_____

_____

2. How does being humble help us to be considerate with another's opinion?

_____

_____

_____

Write out  Galatians 5:26

_____

_____

3. How can being humble help another person see their value?

_____

_____

_____

Write out  Romans 5:8

_____

_____

4. If we are not humble, will it impact our wanting to help others?

_____

_____

_____

Write out  Luke 10:31

_____

_____

# Week Four - Leading

<u>Day Five</u>

*How to be humble.*

1. Does a humble person take all the credit?

_____

_____

_____

Write out  Proverbs 29:23

_____

_____

2. When we are humble should we be willing to listen to criticism?

_____

_____

_____

Write out  Psalm 18:27

_____

_____

3. How does being humble help us to admit we don't know it all?

_____

_____

_____

Write out  2 Chronicles 12:7

_____

_____

4. How can being humble help us to be genuine?

_____

_____

_____

Write out  Romans 12:9

_____

_____

# Leading

## Part Three

## Week Five

## Being Cooperative

# Week Five - Leading

<u>Day One</u>

1. If someone is in a bad mood, how can that affect us?

_____

_____

_____

Write out  Proverbs 29:11

_____

_____

2. Have we ever been pulled into a conflict?

_____

_____

_____

Write out  Luke 22:24

_____

_____

3. How could "re-writing" a conflict we find ourselves in bring resolution?

_____

_____

Write out  2 Timothy 2:23

_____

_____

4. Have we let others affect us? In good or bad ways?

_____

_____

_____

Write out  Matthew 6:24

_____

_____


At the beginning of each week, you will rate yourself concerning these areas – where you are physically, where you are emotionally, and where you are spiritually.

Physically-  1  2  3  4  5  6  7  8  9  10

Emotionally- 1  2  3  4  5  6  7  8  9  10

Spiritually-  1  2  3  4  5  6  7  8  9  10

# Week Five - Leading

<u>Day Two</u>

*Handling conflict Biblically.*

1. Are you a person who tries to handle conflict or run from it?

_____

_____

_____

Write out  1 Corinthians 1:10

_____

_____

2. How can conflict best be handled?

_____

_____

_____

Write out  Matthew 21:12-13

_____

_____

3. How can conflict break up relationships?

_____

_____

_____

Write out  Proverbs 28:25

_____

_____

4. How can we be cooperative to overcome conflict?

_____

_____

_____

Write out  Hebrews 10:24

_____

_____

# Week Five - Leading

<u>Day Three</u>

*We are to help one another.*

1. How do we need each other?

_____

_____

_____

Write out  Genesis 2:18

_____

_____

2. When was a time someone really helped you?

_____

_____

_____

Write out  Hebrews 13:16

_____

_____

3. How much more can we accomplish if we help each other?

_____

_____

Write out  Genesis 11:6

_____

_____

4. Has there been a time when we needed help but didn't ask for it?

Write out  James 4:2

# Week Five - Leading

<u>Day Four</u>

*We can be cooperative with others when we know their strengths.*

1. Are we aware of the strengths or gifts of others?

_____
_____
_____

Write out  Judges 16:6

_____
_____

2. Are we intimidated or jealous of the strengths of others?

_____
_____
_____

Write out  1 Corinthians 3:3

_____
_____

3. Has there been a time when you needed someone's strength but didn't know it?

_____
_____
_____

Write out  1 Corinthians 12:26

_____
_____

4. Has there been a time in your life when someone's advice really helped?

Write out Proverbs 11:14

# Week Five - Leading

<u>Day Five</u>

*It is truly best when we work together.*

1. Do you know the benefits of cooperating together?

_____

_____

_____

Write out  1 Corinthians 3:9

_____

_____

2. What happens if we don't work together?

_____

_____

_____

Write out  Mark 3:25

_____

_____

3. What is the best way to work together?

_____

_____

_____

Write out  Romans 12:16

_____

_____

4. What would you say is one of your God-given strengths, gifts, or abilities?

_____

_____

_____

Write out  1 Peter 4:10

_____

_____

# Leading

## Part Three

## Week Six

## Being Realistic

# Week Six - Leading

<u>Day One</u>

*Having a healthy sense of humor.*

1. How is your sense of humor?

_____

_____

_____

Write out  Job 8:21

_____

_____

2. Can humor help us be realistic?

_____

_____

_____

Write out  Proverbs 10:28

_____

_____

3. Are there any situations in our life we are taking too seriously?

_____

_____

_____

Write out  Psalm 32:11

_____

_____

4. How can humor help during times we might feel overwhelmed ?

_____

_____

_____

Write out  Psalm 71:23

_____

_____

At the beginning of each week, you will rate yourself concerning these areas – where you are physically, where you are emotionally, and where you are spiritually.

Physically- 1  2  3  4  5  6  7  8  9  10

Emotionally- 1  2  3  4  5  6  7  8  9  10

Spiritually- 1  2  3  4  5  6  7  8  9  10

# Week Six - Leading

<u>Day Two</u>

*Seeing the big picture.*

1. What do you think about the statement- This too shall pass?

_____

_____

_____

Write out 1 John 4:1

_____

_____

2. How does looking at the "big picture" help?

_____

_____

_____

Write out Isaiah 40:8

_____

_____

3. How did we get through past challenges?

_____

_____

_____

Write out 1 Samuel 17:47

_____

_____

4. How can you keep doing the right things to get through your challenges?

---

---

---

Write out  Proverbs 28:18

---

---

# Week Six - Leading

<u>Day Three</u>

*Having goals.*

1. How important are goals to us?

_____

_____

_____

Write out  Proverbs 4:25

_____

_____

2. Where will we be in a year?

_____

_____

_____

Write out  Proverbs 24:27

_____

_____

3. Where will we be in five years?

_____

_____

_____

Write out  John 6:27

_____

_____

4. If we ask, do you think God would place a God-sized goal/dream in our heart?

Write out  Psalm 37:4-5

# Week Six - Leading

<u>Day Four</u>

*Anger.*

1. Do you know angry people?

_____
_____
_____

Write out  James 1:20

_____
_____

2. Why do they say they are angry?

_____
_____
_____

Write out  Proverbs 15:18

_____
_____

3. How does their anger teach you not to be angry?

_____
_____
_____

Write out  Proverbs 22:24

_____
_____

4. What is a result of their anger?

Write out  Proverbs 29:11

# Week Six - Leading

<u>Day Five</u>

*What anger can do.*

1. How can anger hurt us physically?

_____
_____
_____

Write out  Proverbs 30:33

_____
_____

2. How can anger lead us to do or say something we will later regret?

_____
_____
_____

Write out  Ephesians 4:26

_____
_____

3. How can anger consume us?

_____
_____
_____

Write out  Proverbs 19:11

_____
_____

4. Does being angry really help in any way?

---

---

---

Write out  Ecclesiastes 7:9

---

---

# Legacy

## Part Four

## Week One

## Relationships

# Week One - Relationships

<u>Day One</u>

*Legacy can be defined as- 1: a gift by will, especially of money or other personal property: a bequest . 2 : something transmitted by or received from an ancestor or predecessor or from the past.*

1. What would you say was a core value you have received from an ancestor or predecessor?

_____

_____

_____

Write out  Proverbs 13:22

_____

_____

2. Why are core values important?

_____

_____

_____

Write out  Proverbs 16:2

_____

_____

3. Are our core values visible for others to see?

_____

_____

_____

Write out  Luke 16:10

_____

_____

4. When we think about our future and the legacy we want to leave, are we aware of how quickly time goes by?

_____

_____

_____

Write out  James 4:14

_____

_____

At the beginning of each week, you will rate yourself concerning these areas – where you are physically, where you are emotionally, and where you are spiritually.

Physically- 1  2  3  4  5  6  7  8  9  10

Emotionally- 1  2  3  4  5  6  7  8  9  10

Spiritually- 1  2  3  4  5  6  7  8  9  10

# Week One - Relationships

<u>Day Two</u>

*The gift of friendship.*

1. How important are the friendships that we make?

_____

_____

_____

Write out  1 Corinthians 15:33

_____

_____

2. How do we nourish a good friendship?

_____

_____

_____

Write out  John 15:13

_____

_____

3. What can sour a friendship?

_____

_____

Write out  2 Corinthians 10:12

_____

_____

4. How could remaining flexible be a benefit to friendships?

Write out  Romans 1:12

# Week One - Relationships

<u>Day Three</u>

*Celebrating Singleness.*

1. Do you think there is pressure put on single women to find that "special someone?"

_____

_____

_____

Write out  Song of Solomon 3:5

_____

_____

2. Why do you think some people consider singleness a "problem?"

_____

_____

_____

Write out  1 Corinthians 7:34-35

_____

_____

3. What would be a way we could make sure single women feel welcome in our circle?

_____

_____

_____

Write out  Psalm 68:6

_____

_____

4. What could we do to offer support to single women we may know?

_____

_____

_____

Write out  Acts 21:9

_____

_____

# Week Two - Relationships

<u>Day Four</u>

*Consider the Widow.*

1. What could be a major challenge for a widowed woman?

_____

_____

_____

Write out  James 1:27

_____

_____

2. What benefit could we be to a widow if we were a safe person to talk to?

_____

_____

_____

Write out  1 Timothy 5:3

_____

_____

3. What would be a way we could include widows into our circle?

_____

_____

_____

Write out  Isaiah 1:17

_____

_____

4. What could we do to offer comfort to widowed women we may know?

_____

_____

_____

Write out  Acts 6:1

_____

_____

# Week One - Relationships

<u>Day Five</u>

*Celebrating Marriage.*

1. Have you ever dreamed of being married?

_____

_____

_____

Write out  Proverbs 18:22

_____

_____

2. Why would someone say that being married is *work*?

_____

_____

_____

Write out  Ephesians 5:33

_____

_____

3. How could looking to your spouse to meet all your needs and keep you happy be unrealistic?

_____

_____

_____

Write out  1 Peter 4:8

_____

_____

4. How can we work through difficulties in marriage?

Write out  Hebrews 13:4

# Legacy

## Part Four

## Week Two

## Walking in Love

# Week Two - Walking in Love

<u>Day One</u>

*The impact of love.*

1. Is there any other force greater than love?

_____
_____
_____

Write out  1 Corinthians 13:13

_____
_____

2. Is love temporary?

_____
_____
_____

Write out  Psalm 100:5

_____
_____

3. How much can love overcome?

_____
_____
_____

Write out  Romans 8:37

_____
_____

4. Have we been called to be loving?

_____

_____

_____

Write out  John 13:35

_____

_____

At the beginning of each week, you will rate yourself concerning these areas – where you are physically, where you are emotionally, and where you are spiritually.

Physically- 1  2  3  4  5  6  7  8  9  10

Emotionally- 1  2  3  4  5  6  7  8  9  10

Spiritually- 1  2  3  4  5  6  7  8  9  10

# Week Two - Walking in Love

<u>Day Two</u>

*Those who have loved us.*

1. Write down two people who have really loved you.

_____

_____

_____

Write out  1 John 3:17

_____

_____

2. What makes you say that they have loved you?

_____

_____

_____

Write out  Ephesians 1:16

_____

_____

3. How easy is it to love?

_____

_____

_____

Write out  Ephesians 5:1-2

_____

_____

4. Have we always been easy to love?

_____

_____

_____

Write out 1 John 4:20-21

_____

_____

# Week Two - Walking in Love

<u>Day Three</u>

*How not to love.*

1. Can we be selfish and still loving?

_____

_____

_____

Write out  James 3:14

_____

_____

2. How can listening to someone make them feel loved?

_____

_____

_____

Write out  Proverbs 12:15

_____

_____

3. What happens to us when we hold a grudge?

_____

_____

_____

Write out  Leviticus 19:18

_____

_____

4. Can we love someone and not be supportive?

_____

_____

_____

Write out  Proverbs 17:17

_____

_____

# Week Two - Walking in Love

<u>Day Four</u>

*Loving ourselves.*

1. Is it okay to love in an abusive way?

_____

_____

_____

Write out  1 Corinthians 13:4-7

_____

_____

2. How do we feel knowing that an abuser can look like a boyfriend, spouse, a boss, or even a trusted friend or family member?

_____

_____

_____

Write out  Psalm 11:5

_____

_____

3. Could abuse be a hopeless situation?

_____

_____

Write out  Romans 15:13

_____

_____

4. How do I love myself if I have experienced an abuse of love?

_____

_____

_____

Write out  Isaiah 54:4

_____

_____

If you or someone you know needs help and guidance concerning abuse, please seek professional help.

Focus on the Family offers a one-time complimentary consultation from a Christian perspective.

Reach a counselor at 1-855-771-HELP (4357)

# Week Two - Walking in Love

<u>Day Five</u>

*Loving ourselves.*

1. Why is it important to love ourselves?

_____

_____

_____

Write out  Mark 12:31

_____

_____

2. How hard is it to receive grace?

_____

_____

_____

Write out  John 15:13

_____

_____

3. How much do we value ourself?

_____

_____

_____

Write out  Ephesians 2:4-5

_____

_____

4. How can lifting others up show them we love and value them?

_____

_____

_____

Write out  John 3:16

_____

_____

# Legacy

## Part Four

## Week Three

## Language of Love

# Week Three - Language of Love

<u>Day One</u>

*Sexuality: it represents some of our greatest vulnerabilities.*

1. Did you receive "The Talk" about sex when you were growing up?

_____

_____

_____

Write out  Genesis 2:24

_____

_____

2. Have you heard the phrase, "Sex sells?"

_____

_____

_____

Write out  1 Corinthians 6:18

_____

_____

3. Can we fall into the trap of twisting sexuality and its holiness?

_____

_____

_____

Write out  1 Thessalonians 4:3

_____

_____

4. How could we keep the sexual side of our being in balance?

_____

_____

_____

Write out  1 Thessalonians 4:7

_____

_____

At the beginning of each week, you will rate yourself concerning these areas – where you are physically, where you are emotionally, and where you are spiritually.

Physically-  1  2  3  4  5  6  7  8  9  10

Emotionally- 1  2  3  4  5  6  7  8  9  10

Spiritually-  1  2  3  4  5  6  7  8  9  10

# Week Three - Language of Love

<u>Day Two</u>

*How to love others.*

1. How can honest dialogue, rather than sarcasm, show we value a person ?

_____
_____
_____

Write out  Proverbs 26:18-19

_____
_____

2. What makes a person put others down?

_____
_____
_____

Write out  Proverbs 18:21

_____
_____

3. How can apologizing demonstrate our love?

_____
_____
_____

Write out  Ephesians 4:32

_____
_____

4. How easy is it to make another look good?

_____

_____

_____

Write out  Philippians 1:7

_____

_____

# Week Three - Language of Love

Day Three

*Being generous.*

*Generosity is defined as : 1. freely giving or sharing money or other valuable things; 2. providing more than the amount that is needed or normal; 3. showing kindness and concern for others.*

1. Have you had someone be generous toward you?

_____

_____

_____

Write out  Acts 20:35

_____

_____

2. Thinking about the most generous person you know, what makes them an inspiring giver?

_____

_____

_____

Write out  Luke 6:38

_____

_____

3.  Are there times when we might have the capacity to give more than we do?

_____

_____

_____

Write out  2 Corinthians 9:7

_____

_____

4. Would you say that generous people seem content?

_____

_____

_____

Write out  1 Timothy 6:7-8

_____

_____

# Week Three - Language of Love

<u>Day Four</u>

*Practicing hospitality.*

*Hospitality is defined as- the friendly and generous reception and entertainment of guests, visitors, or strangers.*

1. How well do we serve others?

_____
_____
_____

Write out  Hebrews 13:2

_____
_____

2. How important is it to make time for someone?

_____
_____
_____

Write out  Acts 28:7

_____
_____

3. How often do we intentionally serve others?

_____
_____
_____

Write out  Acts 16:14-15

_____
_____

4. Is there a difference between hospitality and entertaining?

_____

_____

_____

Write out  Romans 12:13

_____

_____

# Week Three - Language of Love

<u>Day Five</u>

*Those who have shown hospitality to us.*

1. Write down the names of two people who have shown us hospitality.

_____
_____
_____

Write out  Leviticus 19:34

_____
_____

2. Why do you say they were hospitable?

_____
_____
_____

Write out  Titus 1:8

_____
_____

3. How did their hospitality make you feel?

_____
_____
_____

Write out  Romans 16:2

_____
_____

4. How does other's hospitality toward us encourage us to practice hospitality?

_____

---

---

Write out  1 Timothy 5:10

---

---

# Legacy

## Part Four

## Week Four

## Time to Teach

# Week Four - Time to Teach

<u>Day One</u>

*Sharing from experience.*

1. How do we help others when we teach them what we know?

_____
_____
_____

Write out  Proverbs 31:26

_____
_____

2. What if we feel we are not old enough or knowledgeable enough to teach others?

_____
_____
_____

Write out  Psalm 68:11

_____
_____

3. How could teaching others give us a sense of satisfaction?

_____
_____
_____

Write out  Colossians 3:16

_____
_____

4. How could the example of our lives be a teaching tool?

_____

_____

_____

Write out  Titus 2:1

_____

_____

At the beginning of each week, you will rate yourself concerning these areas – where you are physically, where you are emotionally, and where you are spiritually.

Physically-  1  2  3  4  5  6  7  8  9  10

Emotionally- 1  2  3  4  5  6  7  8  9  10

Spiritually-  1  2  3  4  5  6  7  8  9  10

# Week Four - Time to Teach

<u>Day Two</u>

*Those who taught us.*

1. Write down two people who have taught you something.

_____

_____

_____

Write out  Proverbs 22:6

_____

_____

2. What were some of the lessons that you learned from them?

_____

_____

_____

Write out  Romans 12:7

_____

_____

3. How did their lessons impact you?

_____

_____

_____

Write out  2 Thessalonians 2:15

_____

_____

4. Have we taught the lessons we have learned from others in our life?

_____

_____

_____

Write out  Luke 6:40

_____

_____

# Week Four - Time to Teach

<u>Day Three</u>

*What happens if we don't teach.*

1. If we neglect to teach can wisdom be lost?

_____

_____

_____

Write out  Romans 15:4

_____

_____

2. How can teaching others save them from making mistakes?

_____

_____

_____

Write out  Nehemiah 8:8

_____

_____

3. How can not teaching others stop our legacy?

_____

_____

_____

Write out  Philippians 4:9

_____

_____

4. How can not teaching others be a disservice?

_____

_____

_____

Write out  Deuteronomy 6:6

_____

_____

# Week Four - Time to Teach

<u>Day Four</u>

*How to teach.*

1. How can having a specific curriculum help us?

_____

_____

_____

Write out  Matthew 4:23

_____

_____

2. How can having relevant material help in our teaching?

_____

_____

_____

Write out  Acts 15:35

_____

_____

3. How can being passionate when we teach make a difference?

_____

_____

_____

Write out  2 Timothy 3:16-17

_____

_____

4. How can involving others in their lessons help us teach them?

_____

_____

_____

Write out  2 Timothy 2:2

_____

_____

# Week Four - Time to Teach

<u>Day Five</u>

*Practical tips about teaching.*

1. How can knowing the student help us to teach them?

_____

_____

_____

Write out  Romans 10:17

_____

_____

2. How can encouraging questions help us teach people?

_____

_____

_____

Write out  Matthew 16:15

_____

_____

3. How can keeping things clear and understandable help our teaching?

_____

_____

_____

Write out  Acts 28:31

_____

_____

4. How can being genuine help our teaching?

_____

_____

_____

Write out  2 Timothy 3:10

_____

_____

# Legacy

## Part Four

## Week Five

## Thinking to the Future

# Week Five - Thinking to the Future

<u>Day One</u>

*What happens if we don't think of the future?*

1. How easy is it to think negatively about the future?

_____

_____

_____

Write out  Psalm 94:19

_____

_____

2. If we don't think about the future are we missing the big picture?

_____

_____

_____

Write out  2 Corinthians 4:17

_____

_____

3. Can not thinking of the future hinder our personal growth?

_____

_____

_____

Write out  Luke 12:20

_____

_____

4. How does thinking about the future and determining where we are right now, make us focus on what we want to leave as a legacy?

_____

_____

_____

Write out  1 Chronicles 16:11

_____

_____

At the beginning of each week, you will rate yourself concerning these areas – where you are physically, where you are emotionally, and where you are spiritually.

Physically-  1  2  3  4  5  6  7  8  9  10

Emotionally-  1  2  3  4  5  6  7  8  9  10

Spiritually-  1  2  3  4  5  6  7  8  9  10

# Week Five - Thinking to the Future

<u>Day Two</u>

*How to think about the future.*

1. How can learning from our mistakes help us think about the future?

_____

_____

_____

Write out  Proverbs 24:16

_____

_____

2. How can making a mistake cause us to feel trapped?

_____

_____

_____

Write out  Psalm 37:24

_____

_____

3. How do we respond to others when they make a mistake?

_____

_____

_____

Write out  Romans 3:23

_____

_____

4. How do we react when we are the one who makes a mistake?

_____

_____

_____

Write out  Mark 14:72

_____

_____

# Week Five - Thinking to the Future

<u>Day Three</u>

*Manners matter.*

1. How important is it to be polite?

_____

_____

_____

Write out  Titus 3:2

_____

_____

2. How can being respectful be seen as being polite?

_____

_____

_____

Write out  Hebrews 5:2

_____

_____

3. How can remaining respectful reflect that it is not about us?

_____

_____

_____

Write out  Philippians 4:5

_____

_____

4. How can being gentle build others up?

_____

_____

_____

Write out 1 Thessalonians 2:7

_____

_____

# Week Five - Thinking to the Future

<u>Day Four</u>

*Being gentle .*

*One definition for gentle is - having or showing a mild, kind, or tender temperament or character.*

1. Write down two people who have been gentle with you.

_____

_____

_____

Write out  Matthew 11:29

_____

_____

2. Why do you say that they were gentle?

_____

_____

_____

Write out  2 Samuel 22:36

_____

_____

3. How would you say that their gentleness affected you?

_____

_____

_____

Write out  Galatians 5:23

_____

_____

4. Seeing gentleness modeled, how can we be gentle to others?

_____

_____

_____

Write out  2 Timothy 2:24

_____

_____

# Week Five - Thinking to the Future

<u>Day Five</u>

*Shyness.*

1. How might we be gentle with people who are shy?

_____

_____

_____

Write out  1 Thessalonians 5:14

_____

_____

2. How does being gentle with someone not tear them down?

_____

_____

_____

Write out  Isaiah 41:1

_____

_____

3. If we are going to be gentle, how much do we need to know about ourselves?

_____

_____

_____

Write out  Romans 7:15

_____

_____

4. How can gentleness be powerful?

_____

_____

_____

Write out  Proverbs 16:32

_____

_____

# Legacy

## Part Four

## Week Six

## Living Legacy

# Week Six - Living Legacy

<u>Day One</u>

*Making a mark.*

1.  Why would a legacy be important to leave behind?

_____

_____

_____

Write out  Psalm 78:4

_____

_____

2. Can we leave a legacy even if we live a quiet and unspectacular life?

_____

_____

_____

Write out  Psalm 145:4

_____

_____

3. Have you ever written out a personal vision/mission statement?

_____

_____

_____

Write out  Habakkuk 2:2

_____

_____

4. What has been the most important role you have played in your life?

_____

_____

_____

Write out  Proverbs 31:29

_____

_____

At the beginning of each week, you will rate yourself concerning these areas – where you are physically, where you are emotionally, and where you are spiritually.

Physically-  1  2  3  4  5  6  7  8  9  10

Emotionally- 1  2  3  4  5  6  7  8  9  10

Spiritually-  1  2  3  4  5  6  7  8  9  10

# Week Six - Living Legacy

<u>Day Two</u>

*Why appearances matter.*

1. Why is good hygiene important when we are interacting with others?

_____

_____

_____

Write out  Romans 12:1

_____

_____

2. How can having a nice appearance be a good witness?

_____

_____

_____

Write out  Isaiah 61:10

_____

_____

3. Do you feel that women hear a message that their main value is in how they look?

_____

_____

_____

Write out  1 Samuel 16:7

_____

_____

4. Could growing older be a thing we can embrace?

_____

_____

_____

Write out  Proverbs 16:31

_____

_____

# Week Six - Living Legacy

<u>Day Three</u>

*Keeping on track.*

1. How can evaluating priorities and our core values keep us on track for the future?

_____
_____
_____

Write out  Proverbs 16:3

_____
_____

2. Would there be a time when we might need to adjust our core values?

_____
_____
_____

Write out  Proverbs 16:9

_____
_____

3. How can enlisting the help of others help us think about the future?

_____
_____
_____

Write out  Proverbs 19:20

_____
_____

4. How can setting goals help us to think about the future?

_____

_____

_____

Write out  Psalm 20:4

_____

_____

# Week Six - Living Legacy

<u>Day Four</u>

*Maintaining balance.*

1. What happens if our priorities become unbalanced?

_____

_____

_____

Write out  1 Timothy 3:5

_____

_____

2. How can not ministering to our families make us off balance?

_____

_____

_____

Write out  1 John 5:3

_____

_____

3. What might ministering to our family look like?

_____

_____

_____

Write out  Isaiah 54:13

_____

_____

4. Am I unfit for ministry if my child/children are not following Christ?

_____

_____

_____

Write out  Ezekiel 34:16

_____

_____

# Week Six - Living Legacy

<u>Day Five</u>

*Generational legacy.*

1. Do you believe it possible to leave a legacy of our beliefs from generation to generation?

_____
_____
_____

Write out  2 Timothy 1:5

_____
_____

2. Can a legacy be lost?

_____
_____
_____

Write out  Judges 2:10

_____
_____

3. Is leaving a legacy inevitable?

_____
_____
_____

Write out  Proverbs 13.22

_____
_____

4. What are we doing right now to create a legacy that we are hopeful to pass on?

_____

_____

_____

Write out  Joshua 4:21-22

_____

_____

# CONGRATULATIONS!

# MAY

# GOD

# RICHLY

# BLESS YOU!

# ABOUT THE AUTHOR

Cris Jacobs' years leading women's groups, studies, and ministering to women of all ages, have given her insights she shares in her book, *Women Mentoring Women*. Serving as a co-director at a crisis pregnancy center for the last 7 years has allowed Cris to offer emotional support and assistance to those at their most vulnerable. Faith and family are what define her. She is happiest when cooking for her husband of 46 years or decorating a birthday cake for her two daughters or one of her six grandchildren.

Manufactured by Amazon.ca
Bolton, ON

34019296R00151